Having Fun with God

A
Book Report
For
Miss. Winfrey

By
Martika Whylly

BALBOA.
PRESS

A DIVISION OF HAY HOUSE

Balboa Press books may be ordered through booksellers or by contacting:

Balboa Press
A Division of Hay House
1663 Liberty Drive
Bloomington, IN 47403
www.balboapress.com
1 (877) 407-4847

Printed in the United States of America.

ISBN: 978-1-4525-9131-5 (sc)
ISBN: 978-1-4525-9132-2 (e)

Balboa Press rev. date: 2/28/2014

This story is based on my experiences. Some of the names have been changed to protect the privacy of those involved.

I know who I am
I know where I'm from
I know what I'm capable of and
I know how to overcome

For Marilyn

Introduction

I was having the time of my life at the summer music festival. The celebration was an auspicious event and the sun was shining bright even though an overcast of large clouds slowly rolled in. It looked like it was going to rain, but it didn't. People from all over were drawn towards the vibrant sounds of the three live bands that hummed synchronism; harmonizing a few hundred yards away from each other. The music was calling so loud, I could feel my heart pounding in sequence with the thick pulsing sounds of thunder, coming from a bass drum; Roaring, making its way for the percussions. Then blazing electric guitar and harmonic horns were thrown in the mix. Milling through the crowd, intoxicating smells of barbequed foods made my mouth water and the closer I got to any band, the denser the area with hot sweaty bodies moving around making it hard for me to see. There were all kinds of music to choose from, and a full line up of musicians that were yet to have their moment on stage; that I couldn't help bumping into people, as I danced from one venue to another. Smiling faces were everywhere and a great presence of unity flowed through the multitude of people. Everyone was singing, dancing and having fun. Being happy, joyful, feeling euphoric. It truly was a beautiful summer day.

Looking around to see if I recognized anyone, I happened to notice a dark figure, over there, far away in the distance. So far in fact, it appeared as a small dot, blending in the crowd, hanging there suspended amongst a field of bright colors. That's odd. It was looking at me in a mischievous way, perhaps plotting to take my life away. I cringed, turning towards the stage, reassuring myself that I was in my happy place. What harm could come my way? Just then, an incredibly horrifying feeling came over me, and my body started to shiver, shake and vibrate as a thrilling chill moved through me. Filled with fear, I wanted to be as far away as possible from the dark figure, so I fled the scene.

I showed up at a friend's beautifully furnished condo. We had finished a lovely meal, and then went into the living room for drinks and conversation. I leaned back in a big comfy chair, and began to relax holding a glass of white wine. Being in the secured company of loving friends eased my mind from; the dark figure that was opening the front door, entering the living room and staring directly at me. He was a faceless man dressed in black, wearing a hat and reeked of rotten corpses. Gripped with fear and overwhelmed by the stench, I froze. So many questions rushed at me. Why? Why me? Why now? Struggling to get out of the room, I somehow managed to get up and move.

Panicking, I caught up with another old friend, and begged for help. Receiving no console, I tried to explain why I could not stay. "I have to keep going or else the man in black would surely find me and take me away!" The distance between us was rapidly disappearing and I could feel him getting much closer, so I ran and ran and hopelessly, I ran some more. He was right behind me. Realizing there was nowhere else to hide; I stopped running, and turned around to confront him.

"What do you want from me!?" I pleaded. Giving no response, he bent slightly forward with both arms stretched out, pointing his hands down at my feet, slowly wiggling his fingers towards my head and up. As he was doing this, I could feel the energy move up from the bottom of my feet, through my body, to the top of my head and out. It was quick and painless. Still standing and breathing, I wondered to myself, 'That's it?' "That's it," he shrugged. Then he left me alone to chase after someone else.

I stood immobilized, feeling greatly relieved as the fear left, leaving in its place a glorious sensation of peace and harmony. Followed by a bewilderment of what just happened. Dazed, I looked over as the other person was running away from him. Knowing what it's like to die, I wanted to tell her; there's nothing to fear, no need to cry.

****

I awoke early. The sun was peering over the horizon, shining brighter than ever before. I tried to forget the frightening dream or what it might mean. I opened and walked through the French doors to my room and passed Kevin's room, an unoccupied guest's room and then his daughter's Nikki's room. Hearing neither of my cousins stirring, I went up the stairs and into the kitchen to make breakfast. "Good morning, it's another beautiful day", Uncle Pat sang, as he emerged out of the master bedroom and into the living room followed by Aunt Irene. "Mornin." I acknowledged somberly. "Are you working on set today?" Aunt Irene asked. "Yea, Dawn of the Dead, a remake of the classic horror flick." I said. We discussed the movie briefly, then segued into politics. "You know speaking of horrors, I had a nightmare last night and I haven't had a nightmare since I was a little kid." I mentioned. "Oh really, what was it about?" They wanted to know. So, I told them.

"Well it sounds like you conquered your fears head on", Uncle Pat said. "...victoriously facing death itself." Aunt Irene agreed. Although their words were comforting, I was still haunted by the images and the way they made me feel. The dream was so real. I hope that's all it means, overcoming my fears. Even though it was morning, I could still feel his dark presence and the thrilling chill he gave as he chased me in my sleep. It had me staring into space as I sat at the kitchen table. I tried to shrug it off. It was just a dream. Besides, it was a beautiful summer day and being assured that I had conquered death, what harm could possibly come my way?

"You haven't been tampering in the shed out back have you?" Uncle Pat asked interrupting my thoughts. "No," I said. "Why do you ask?" "Well it looks like someone's been in there moving things around. I fixed it so no one goes in." he replied. I wondered why I was being questioned but said nothing more, then told them to have a good day and went downstairs. I showered, changed, hopped in my ride and switched radio stations until I found a song that I liked. 'Sunday bloody Sunday' by U2 was playing again, I must have heard it a hundred times this week already. '...I can't believe the news today, I can't close my eyes and make it go away....' Pulling out of the driveway, I sped down the windy road with a cigarette in my hand and headed towards the city.

The set was located in downtown Toronto at an old abandoned factory mill by the lake, just off Lakeshore Blvd. on Cherry Street. Worn down, dusty old buildings made for the perfect zombie shot. We were at that spot for about a week, then on to the mall. It was August 2003, I'll never forget that summer. We extras would show up between 6 and 8am and sign in at the table they set up in the tent, called extra's holding. Then go to wardrobe, hair and makeup. Since the background extras (about a hundred of us) were playing zombies we came in our own clothes that we didn't mind getting ruined. Once everyone went through hair and make-up, we looked hideous. We teased and joked with each other about it at first, acting like crazed monsters was time well spent, including getting a kick out of scaring the looky loos. Finally, they were ready for us on set. In this scene, they had us running down the street, in the heat, chasing after the main characters that were getting away in a beat up old van. After doing each scene a few times, I started to imagine that I was running in a race, and when the director called "Cut!" I yelled, "I won, I won, I won, zombie racing is lots of fun!", while waving my arms in the air. Giggling, I walked back to first position, as some of the crew were amused by my antics.

A few days into filming we experienced a black out. A power outage that effected not only Toronto but most of the eastern seaboard down to Florida and as far west as Winnipeg, so I heard. Since being on location means trailers, battery charged cameras, generators for equipment and air conditioning the tent, the power being off didn't affect us at all. In fact, we didn't find out until much later when the 3rd A.D. came into the extras holding to make an announcement. "Ok folks, your attention for a moment. Just to let you know what's going on in the world apart from our own world. The power is out in the city and in most of the eastern seaboard. It's been out since four o'clock it is now six. They don't know what caused it but are working on it according to the news/media. I'll do my best to keep you posted. Thanks for your attention." Then he left.

I relaxed in my portable lounge chair thinking, 'I'm glad I filled up this morning, at least I can get home.' I tried calling family and friends to find out how they were doing, but all the circuits were busy. I sensed that everyone was ok, although some radio stations that had back up power were describing the black out as chaotic. Traffic being out of control as a result of everyone going home all at once; but some people came together to help direct the mesh of cars at main intersections. Others

9

were stranded and had to rely on public transit, which was also a mess. Meanwhile the lost sense of security prompted many storeowners to sit in front of their shops to prevent looters from stealing. People were selling flashlights for 20 dollars and on it went. I dozed off. An hour later, I got out of my chair and wandered out to see where they were in the scene and how long it would be before they used us again. "Not long." The 3rd A.D. said looking at his sides, "We're here until the sunsets." Then he hurried off speaking into his headset. We continued filming until 9pm using generated powered lights. Filming a horror in the middle of a black out, not just here but everywhere seemed to be an eerie coincidence some of us thought.

"Ok people that's a wrap!" shouted the 3rd A.D. "Don't forget your call times for tomorrow before you sign out. Thank you!" We were herded back to the tent while the makeup crew came around with wet cloths to remove the makeup from our faces. We weren't allowed to go home looking like zombies; too bad for me because

I wanted to scare the living crap out of Nikki. Maybe that would cheer her up since things with her boyfriend weren't going so well. Aunt Irene gave her a cute kitten, that Nikki named Shorty, hoping the affectionate pet would bring her some happiness.

'Next time I'll get her,' I thought smiling to myself. I signed out, walked over to my car, drove onto the dark and quiet avenue and headed towards the Gardiner Expressway. The only movement I could see was the images of people walking down the street. The darkness had everyone appearing as zombies. Straining to see what was in front of me, I drove through several streetlights, not seeing them until after I passed an intersection. Everyone had gone home; there were few cars around and even fewer cars on the highway. A rare sight for a Thursday night, the city resembled a ghost town. My only concern was whether we had power. Pushing in a Missy Elliot CD I turned up the music, eased back in my seat and enjoyed having the highway all to myself. As I drove further away, passing the James Snow Parkway cut off, there were still no signs of electricity.

Darkness followed me home and it was just Kevin and I in the house. We talked about all the reasons why the massive power outage occurred. I really wanted to bathe and get the rest of the dirt and makeup off. Dust, sweat and fake blood had settled on my skin, and my hair was all caked up with red colored hair gel. Kevin asked me to help conserve water, by waiting to shower when the power came back on. I reluctantly agreed, that meant sleeping in zombie filth. Although it could've been worse, I was not impressed with the situation.

Halleluiah! It was Friday, and the lights were back on. That was the first thing I noticed when I woke up. I jumped in the shower before anyone else could get into the bathroom and came out feeling like a new person all squeaky clean. Even though it meant being clean for only a few hours because I was back on set only to go through the same routine of being converted from a human being into a zombie with the magic of hair and makeup. The day seemed to race by and before I knew it, the weekend had arrived.

Carrie invited me to her cousin's scavenger hunt party up north on Saturday. It was a two-hour drive. Everyone had plans to be out of town except Nikki. I asked her if she wanted to come to the scavenger hunt party but she declined. I didn't know what she had planned but she usually spent most of her time with her boyfriend or with friends doing her own thing, since she was fifteen. Instead I brought Blue our beautiful husky, at the request of my aunt. I had mixed feelings about going, I wanted to see my friends but oddly enough wasn't in the partying mood.

The scavenger hunt meant driving from one location to another to collect items such as finding a particular rock in a field or going to Hooters and filling out an application. We were placed in teams of three and the first team to get everything on the list and return home – wins. We played and drove around for a few hours. I was getting bored quick and just wanted to relax a bit. When the game ended we all met up at the house, the guys got the barbeque going while the girls set the table putting out the salads, buns, condiments and utensils. I only had one beer with my meal when my stomach started to react. Throughout the course of the evening, I went to the bathroom a few times to yak. I couldn't figure out what was wrong with me, pregnancy was out of the question or maybe it was because I hadn't eaten all day. Anyway, I continued feeling lousy and decided not to stay, even though home was a long drive away.

It was dark when I left and when I reached the main highway, I accelerated to 160 km an hour to get home faster. Even though it was still early, I began feeling very sleepy. Probably due to all the puking and the lack of food depleted my energy. I turned the radio up and winded the window all the way down to let the coolness of the night breeze blow on my face. I thought it might help but my eyelids grew heavy, heavier and heavier still, then closed just for a moment. When I reopened them, I was veering off to the left side of the highway heading towards the center guardrail. The car started swerving out of control as I struggled to regain consciousness when a sudden jolt within, made me jerk the car back onto the lane. Fully alert and frantically breathing, I glanced back to see if Blue was ok. The near death experience caused the adrenaline to pump through my veins. Calming myself, I was able to reach home safe and sound, and went straight to bed.

I was in a deep sleep when the sound of Blue's howling woke me up. It was midday when I finally heard her. Feeling somewhat rested from the night before, I rolled out of bed, quickly dressed, grabbed her leash and was out the door. I wished at that time I had a wagon to sit in and have her lead me like a husky sled. Because she was sprinting down the driveway so fast, pulling me hard giving my arm whiplash. I was immediately thrown into a jog. When I came back from the run, I gave her food and fresh water. Hunger began to build inside me as well. I went into my room, made the bed, washed up and started to think about what to make for dinner once everyone got home. My thoughts were invaded by loud talking coming from Nikki's room. "Why are you doing this to me?" she repeated over and over again crying. "So a year didn't mean anything to you?" she yelled, then threatened "I'll do something you'll regret, I mean it!" She was on the phone with her boyfriend and it appeared as though he was breaking up with her. She was really upset by the sound of it, and not taking rejection too well. I wanted to comfort her. She emerged from her room with tears in her eyes; I asked if she was ok. "Yea" she replied. She didn't want to talk about it, then passed me and headed outside. I felt helpless in the situation. I asked her to come with me to the grocery store, not wanting to leave her alone in that state, she said "No". "I know you're upset, let's talk, come with me please." I asked her again but she refused to co-operate. She came back in the house and reentered her room only to call her boyfriend back and continue to argue. "Why are you doing this to me? I swear I'll do something you'll regret!" she threatened again. As I stood watching the drama unfold, contemplating on what to do, a surging hunger pang ripped through my stomach. I couldn't ignore the pain any longer, so I grabbed a banana and ate it as I drove to the grocery store.

I hadn't planned to be gone long but I got a call from a friend that I hadn't seen in awhile, wanting to know what I was up to, and asked if I wouldn't mind stopping by. After shopping, I visited for about an hour or so, than left for home to start preparing dinner. It was a quarter after 6 when I got home. Nikki's door was closed, and I assumed she had gone out again since I didn't hear any yelling coming from her room. I went into the kitchen and started getting dinner ready and called my aunt and uncle to see what time they would be coming home. Aunt Irene said they were on their way and asked if I had heard from Kevin, their son, when I heard the cries of Shorty, Nikki's kitten coming from her room. I went back downstairs, opened the door slightly, and Shorty bolted out. The light in her room was left on and I didn't see her and figured she'd gone out after putting some pictures and a letter that was neatly placed on the floor in the center of her room. I glanced at it and closed the door. I walked back upstairs followed by Shorty and gave her some cat food that she ate in a hurry then kept my company while I continued cooking.

Dinner was ready and everyone was home. We sat around the kitchen table and discussed current events and how everyone's weekend went. "Where's Nikki?" Aunt Irene inquired. No one knew probably over at her friend's house, we all assumed. I told them what had happened earlier with Nikki and her boyfriend breaking up and Aunt Irene agreed to speak with her. Looking at the time, I excused myself from the table while they were still eating. Aunt Irene asked if I would be so kind as to put Shorty back in Nikki's room. I complied, scooping up the little ball of fur with one hand, and trotted down the stairs.

As I entered her room about to put Shorty down, looking at the pictures that were lying on the floor when something in the corner of my eye caught my attention. I looked up into her closet not believing my eyes. I jumped back and shrieked loudly unconsciously dropping the kitten from my hand. There she was, hanging in the closet underneath the stairs, with an extension cord wrapped around her neck. My first impulse was to take her down but I could see her face was blue, she was dead. Horrified by the sight I flew up the stairs.

Everyone had heard me scream and was looking at me with grave concern. Before anyone could ask, I blurted. "Please go down stairs and tell me I didn't see what I saw!" The screeching sound of the legs on all three chairs scratched the kitchen floor as everyone got up and hurried downstairs. I followed but refused to reenter her room. The looks on their faces was enough confirmation that what I had witnessed was terribly true. Aunt Irene felt her arm. "She's dead," she said. Then began to wail, "Why, why, why, Nikki why!?" Kevin found the note on the floor and began reading it, half mumbling it to himself.

We sat on the couch my aunt and I as I tried to comfort her while she continued wailing, "Why, Nikki, why?" Kevin sat stunned. Uncle Pat called the police. I didn't want to believe it or accept it. I never thought that she meant it or would do such a thing to herself. It puzzled me immensely.

****

I was sitting in my car in front of the library, building the nerve to go in. But every time I blinked my eyes, I could see her blue face while 'Sunday Bloody Sunday' played over and over in my head. '...I can't believe the news today. I can't close my eyes and make it go away. How long, how long must we sing this song? How long? How long?... tonight, we can be as one tonight, tonight. Sunday bloody Sunday, Sunday bloody Sunday...'

She died on Sunday. Why hadn't I seen the signs before? Blaming myself I sat there crying for hours. I felt as if I was forced to look at her in order to make sense of it all. She was hanging there like a rag doll. Another innocent child gave up her life. Why? The song continued playing '...we eat and drink while tomorrow they die...' hanging there waiting to be found while we ate supper. '...Sunday bloody Sunday...Sunday bloody Sunday...' Sobbing profusely, my eyes became stingy and red. '...Wipe the tears from your eyes, wipe your tears away, Sunday bloody Sunday...'

Taking long deep breaths to ease my mind, I closed my eyes and studied her. Her long, straight brown hair was pulled back into a ponytail, her eyes were closed looking peaceful, and there was a serene glow around her head. I prayed that wherever she was, she was happy and free from whatever misery she had locked away in her soul.

Viewing zombies all week and seeing her dead limp body confused and taunted me. The eerie thing about it was I told Nikki I was planning to scare her in my zombie outfit. Instead I managed to swipe my photo from hair and makeup, and showed her the picture of me all gross looking. Nikki merely smiled at it.

She sure outsmarted me by showing her zombie outfit. The jokes on me, because I could see Nikki on the other side, watching and laughing at me, belly over in hysterics. While Vincent Price laughs along with her, hearing his infamous cackle. 'Ah ha ha ha ha, Ah ha ha ha ha...' Echoing in my head. My mind bent and stretched for truth, and the only conclusion I came to was that; God has a really weird sense of humor.

Part One

Hello. My name is Martika Whylly. Martika is derived from the name, Maria. My mom told me Martika means sweet Maria. My father gave me the name and was an entertainer from the Bahamian Islands, and my mother a Canadian tourist on holiday with friends when they met. My dad must have put on a good show and my mom must have enjoyed it because they got married on December 22, 1967. I was conceived in '69, and born on February 26, 1970 to Marilyn Moreau and Deacon Whylly in Nassau, Bahamas. In those days it was rare to see interracial couples. My mom must've really loved my father because her decision to marry and live in the

Bahamas posed a great challenge for her strict, catholic parents to accept.

Growing up, I don't remember much about my father. My parents divorced when I was three and my mom moved back to Toronto with me. We stayed in a cozy one bedroom apartment on Thorncliff Park Ave. Even though there were two single beds in the bedroom, my mom chose to sleep on the sofa bed in the living room. I asked her why she didn't want to share the bedroom. She answered, "Because, it's your room." So I decorated the other bed that leaned against the wall with all my stuffed animals and dolls. In the morning, she would make breakfast and get me dressed. Then drop me off at the daycare center located below the library that was next door while she worked at an office nearby. In the evenings, after eating dinner and watching TV, she'd bathe me and get me ready for bed. Bath time was my favorite. My mom always had a hard time getting me in the tub and an even harder time getting me out. I'd come out of the tub naked and wet, and escape her grasp by pretending to be a frog, hopping on all fours saying, "Ribbit, ribbit." She'd play along and chase me into my room. Then she'd dry me off, help me into my pajamas and tuck me in pretending to be the cookie monster. "Argh, I'm gonna eat you up," she'd tease with kisses.

On weekends she would sleep in. Saturday mornings I would get up early, go into the living room, turn on the TV and quietly watch my favorite cartoon 'The Bugs Bunny and Road Runner show,' until she got up. On Sunday mornings, when there weren't any cartoons, I'd entertain myself. One Sunday morning, I felt like doing somersaults. My bed wasn't wide enough so I decided to use the sofa bed in the living room instead, except my mom was still sleeping in it. No problem, I put some extra pillows over her so she wouldn't feel anything. Rolling over her once, twice and even faster the third time. She was still sleeping. Good. The extra pillows were definitely working. I giggled and continued doing somersaults until I accidentally cut my leg on the jagged side of the bed where the metal protrudes. I looked at the deep cut that started to bleed and began crying. Only then did my mom wake up, wondering why I was crying and why she was covered in pillows.

   She kept a photo album of family pictures among my baby pictures and of their wedding day. The black and white photo of my parents as bride and groom was taken outside of a church. Mom wore white gloves with a simple white sleeveless dress, which curtsey just above her knees. On her feet were closed toe, white sling back two inch heels and her brown hair was neatly pulled back to accentuate her massive bun. Dad had a small afro and wore a dark suit and tie that made him look debonair. There were many baby pictures of me making a variety of facial expressions, arranging in different poses, that she neatly placed in chronological order. As I grew older, I asked her why she didn't want to talk about the people she knew in the Bahamas. "When there isn't anything nice to say, say nothing at all." She replied. I asked her a lot of questions about the pictures, receiving only vague answers. I often wondered about my mom, who she was.

There was mystery about her. Like she knew something and wasn't telling.

Two years later we moved around the corner on Don Mills road in a two bedroom apartment on the eighth floor of a twenty six storey building. It was great because it had a variety store in the basement and an outdoor swimming pool in the back. I made friends with the other kids that lived in the building. In the winter, we would go tobogganing outside and play Nicky-Nicky nine door inside and in the summer we would be in the pool as soon as it opened and stayed until it closed. We made friends with the lifeguard and would eat lunch together on the lawn, picnic style each day when the pool closed for an hour. My mom never had to worry about a babysitter.

Friday's were special because it was pay day. That's when we all got our allowances. My mom would give me five dollars and my friends and I would pig out at McDonald's then go to the variety store and get hyper on candy.

When I was seven, my father showed up and ended up staying for a week or so. I wasn't sure why he came but I was glad to see him. My mom gave me permission to stay home from school for a day to spend more time with him. I set up a small chalkboard in the living room and we played school. I was the teacher and he was the pupil. The only question he asked was to go to the bathroom.

He talked my mom into coming back because around that time she planned a trip for us to go to Nassau for three weeks. I was so happy because I hoped they would get back together, and excited about going back home.

Once we arrived in Nassau, Deacon, the man known as my father showed up at the airport, with a blonde woman who was sitting in the front seat of the car. I'm grateful that my mom decided to stay and not turn around and fly back the same day. I would have been furious, so we ended up staying for only a week. In that short period of time, I got to see my father's limbo dancing show, mom and I visited with her friends. I went swimming in the ocean, the pool and spent a couple of days with my cousins at my aunt and uncle's house.

My happy bubble burst, when we arrived back on Canadian soil. I knew there was no chance of reconciling, anything. We made the best of our lives though. She worked as a secretary, while I went to school. In the evenings she helped me with my homework and we would watch TV together. Her favorite program was the Mary Tyler Moore show, mine was Sesame Street. Sometimes our shows came on at the same time, so we'd debate over which one to watch. I usually got my way, being the only child. However, my mom would put on her sad face and give an award winning performance. Ironically, I ended up watching more Mary Tyler Moore shows than Sesame Street. Also, whenever a scary movie came on I'd snuggle up to her. She would always make me jump by saying "Boo!" right when something horrible was about to happen. "Stop it mom!" I'd say angrily. She'd laugh and I'd pout during the commercials, then I'd forget about it and zone into the story again. I enjoyed the times we spent together. Once in awhile we'd go out for dinner and a movie. We were always going places and doing things. She also took me to the Circus, Sesame Street on ice and the Royal Ontario Museum to see the King Tut exhibit.

My friend Ally who lived next door taught me how to ride her bicycle. When she wasn't riding it, I'd hop on and convince her to teach me. She'd run aside me and hold the back part of the seat supporting my balance while I wobbled along. We'd practice after school and kept practicing until I got it. She was a great teacher. Once I mastered the art of bike riding, I followed my mom around the apartment going on and on about how I could ride. "Can I please have a bike?" I persisted. Her answer was maybe, which meant no in my mind. I didn't get everything I wanted, so whenever I thought I wasn't going to get something, I'd turn to God the father and pray earnestly.

One day my mom picked me up from the local community center where I'd go after school and brought me to a department store and she told me to choose a bicycle. I was ecstatic with joy and excitement, because it wasn't even my birthday. I promised her that I'd always ride it, when she asked. My first bicycle was blue with a sparkly banana seat. It was the happiest day of my life. That bike and I became inseparable. Since I managed to get a bike from my mom maybe she'd be willing to make me a little brother or sister to play with. When I asked, she said she didn't want any more children. So I asked for a puppy or kitten to play with. Her answer was always no. Sulking, I'd go to my room and ask God the father instead.

Sasha, a girl who lived in the building was holding a cute kitten in front of her. She couldn't keep him because of her allergies and had to give him away. A few kids had gathered around but none of them were allowed to keep the kitten. I was glad because I knew once my mom saw his little face; she'll surely let me have him. My friends followed me back home to ask my mom for permission. I took the kitten from Sasha and let her hold him. "Please mom, can I keep him?"

Looking at the cute kitten that was shoved in her hand, she sighed. "Okay, but you're responsible for him. You feed him and clean up after him." "I will." I promised. After the show was over and everyone cleared out I asked her. "What name should we give him?" "How about Mickey?" she said. "Mickey's a mouse not a cat." I protested. Then she put on her sad face which got me every time. "Ok, Mickey it is."

I loved playing with him and made up a game by tying a bunched up plastic bag on the end of a string. Then I'd throw it over the side of my bed and he would pounce on the bag, digging his teeth and claws into the plastic. Pulling him up on the string, I squealed. "Look what I caught!" Then give him kisses and do it again.

Around that time the hit song 'Mickey' came out. I would sing that song to Mickey all the time and dance with him. "...O Mickey you're so fine. You're so fine you blow my mind. Hey Mickey... Hey Mickey!" A few weeks later my mom noticed that I was sneezing a lot and wondered if it was because of Mickey. She took me to Sunnybrook Hospital to get tested for allergies. The doctor stuck me with twenty needles in my left arm. After she was done, I felt extremely light headed and had to lie down. I rested, as we waited for the results. When the doctor came back she informed us that while I didn't have any serious reactions to anything. "You are allergic to dust, grass, dead leaves and cat fur."

On the drive home my mom said causally "We might have to give Mickey away." I was not having any of it. "If I stop sneezing can I keep him?" "We'll see." She said. The minute we arrived home I went to my room, stared at myself in the mirror and stated, "I am not allergic to cats." I must've repeated it ten times or until I convinced myself that I was no longer allergic to cats. Miraculously the sneezing stopped and the matter was dropped.

My mom started dating again. I was nine going on ten, when she brought home a man she worked with. His name was Michael. I didn't like him; something about him wasn't gelling with me. I didn't like most of the men she went out with. He was tall about 6'5, medium build with short, straight brown hair, wore glasses and a moustache. He was French Canadian and splitting up with his wife at the time. My mom dated him for two years before they got married. During those seemingly wonderful couple of years we did family things on weekends with his two children; Raine and TJ. It was great having a brother and sister to play with. I would look forward to playing with them both but since they were a brother and sister that lived together, they didn't want to play with each other. So naturally, I joined in on the sibling rivalry. Every other week, they would come to visit. I'd play with TJ and help him pick on Raine. The following weekend I'd play with Raine and help her pick on TJ. It was great because they hardly picked on me.

After my mom and Michael got married, we moved into a bigger apartment in the same building on the twentieth floor, apt. 2010, with a magnificent view of the city. That's when the beatings and verbal abuse began. My mom never wanted to talk about it, even when we were alone. I on the other hand did. But to who, since she was in complete denial. I knew it was only a matter of time before things would get worse. So I asked Raine about her father. She admitted that he had displayed violent behavior towards them, when her parents were together and that was why her mother left him. I wondered why my mom was putting up with him. I told my sister that I loved her but hated her father. Raine understood how I felt, she told me she loved her father but hated his behavior.

I didn't understand it at first. Why would my stepfather want to beat on someone else? Weakness, he was a weak man, I concluded for myself. I learned his father used to beat on him, so he was only following tradition, he didn't know any better. Now knowing and experiencing are two different things. I knew why he was abusive but how does a twelve year old handle that situation?

One night we were sitting at the table, eating dinner and there was this one dish he liked very much that had nuts in it. (My mom prepared meals he liked.) It was sautéed green beans with slivered almonds. I liked the vegetables but I didn't like the almonds. The first time she made it I tried it but didn't like it so I wasn't going to eat it, maybe before Brutus showed up. I attempted to eat the nuts, but there were so many that, I put some in my napkin as I wiped my mouth, then discreetly tucked my dirty napkin along side of the plate. I was all done and about to get up, when Michael said, "Let me see your napkin". Hesitating, I presented the nut filled napkin. I don't remember what else he said. I think I was too scared at that point. He began hitting me, I ran and he chased me around the living room. My mom sat there helplessly.

A week later I was getting out of the tub before going to bed when I heard him beating on her in the living room, and yelling about something. I quickly went into my room and became fuming mad that he was hitting my mom and I couldn't do anything about it. I pounded my fist on the dresser and took my plastic hair brush and whipped it at the wall with all my might. The brush broke into pieces. It was loud enough to get his attention. He came running into

my room, saying something like "What's your problem?"
I don't know what else he said because I was too busy
running around the room, trying to get away from his fist.

After that, whenever he wanted to beat me and was
coming at me, I headed for the front door and started
down the stairs. He never chased me out of the apartment.
That was how I got out of the beatings, but he found other
ways to abuse me when he saw that I could outrun him. He
resorted to verbal threats of physical punishment, until
one day I fired back. "How would you like it, if I did the
same to you?" He towered over me and snarled, "Yea,
you and what army?" Venting with anger and frustration,
I went to my room and asked God to send an army to
protect me and my mom.

My mom wasn't seriously religious, though she took me
to church on Sundays. Michael came sometimes but it was
mainly the two of us going. I found mass incredibly boring
so I daydreamed through most of it. Often wondering why
priests weren't allowed to marry or have sex. Clearly

God gave us sexual feelings for a reason. I thought the whole matter; queer.

On holidays, we would watch 'Jesus of Nazareth' or 'The Ten Commandments' depending on the time of year. In those movies, my favorite part was the beautiful mysterious beings from heaven known as Angels. I secretly prayed for an Angel to appear to me, just like the one in 'Our lady of Light'.

On a lovely Sunday morning, May 13, 1917, three young shepherd children in Portugal saw a beautiful lady appear before them, shining brighter than the sun.*

One night while I was sleeping, I rose out of my body and I could see myself in bed, it was the strangest thing. Then a brilliant white light bathed and washed over me. I began to shiver when a tranquil voice from the light said, "Do not be afraid". My fear disappeared. I looked towards the light as he continued to speak, giving a profound message. I clearly heard each word that was spoken, but as I tried to retrieve them, they melted and fell away into my core being. "Do not be afraid" the voice from the light said again, and faded away.

I awoke from a cool breeze and got up to close the window in awe. I tried very hard to remember the words, but none came to mind, leaving only a feeling of wonder. I went to my mom about it the next day. We were alone in my room. I was sitting on my bed while she knelt on the carpeted floor in front of me. I told my mom of the experience in as much detail as I could. "What did the Angel say?" she asked. Bowing my head, I said. "I can't remember, only 'Do not be afraid'". She bowed her head as well. "I believe you" she said softly. Then she told me to let her know if it happens again.

The Angel experience I'm sharing with you is dedicated to my friend Margaret, who encouraged me to write about it and also for Oprah Winfrey. (If you will please excuse this little detour.)

I was first introduced to Oprah when she played Sofia in 'The Color Purple'. I loved her character because she was a smart, hardworking, determined, strong, and a very outspoken woman. I often dreamt about meeting Miss. Winfrey because she is a positive role model in my life. I didn't see all of her shows, but I'd watch whenever I could. She had become more of a mother figure to me over the years, than just a figure on TV. I heard a woman say on her show that; 'Oprah is a TV mom for many of us, because she has helped so many through so much.' Like a real nurturing caregiver. That's why she is so rich...so full of love. As her popularity grew, I felt my chances of ever meeting her slowly diminish. Had I become like many of those who doubted themselves into further denial and self pity? Yes, but I always overcame such thoughts, by reading personal growth/self help and inspirational books.

I remember Oprah telling her audience, when she was a little girl in school, she handed in a book report much earlier than the due date and became the main discussion in the teachers' lounge. I must have heard that story on more than one occasion. About the third or fourth time hearing it, I began thinking maybe God's trying to tell me something. "Yea, Write a book about your life experiences, and share it." I didn't think I could write a book, let alone a book report for Miss. Winfrey. Even though she's always promoting books and encouraging people to read and write. I thought. Why not? So I convinced myself that I could do it. It would have to be an A plus kind of read so I took my time and asked God for help. I started to think about where to begin, when my thoughts led me to my earliest school memories; Kindergarten, where my learning began...

I got in trouble for fighting during recess, because of this one boy who was spitting on me. When I retaliated, he told the teacher. The teacher scolded me in front of everyone and I was removed from the class and put into another.

In grade one, I punched a girl in the arm when she wouldn't let me play with my doll that I forgot to bring

41

home after taking it to school for show and tell. When the teacher turned off the lights to indicate quiet time, everyone stopped what they were doing, but the little girl kept on crying. That got me transferred into another class as well. I was always in trouble for something. By the end of the fourth grade my mom decided to move me out of St. John XXIII and into another catholic school, St. Bonaventure. It was two bus rides away. After that I didn't fight anymore.

Needless to say I didn't like school very much and hated doing homework. My mind wandered often and as a result was a "C" average student all the way up through high school. Most of my teachers' notes read something like, "Martika is easily distracted and likes to talk. She is smart and can easily improve her grades with more study." Unlike Oprah I had to make a great effort when it came to school.

To be honest, my first book report was never written. I just started the fifth grade in the new school and our teacher, Miss. Shannon gave the class a book report assignment. I was too embarrassed to ask what a book report was, so I didn't do it. The morning the assignment was due, I was worried sick. In class Miss. Shannon asked everyone to place their report on her desk, then she turned to write on the blackboard. I was grateful that I was not singled out as to where mine was but I was sure to be questioned when she discovers it missing. A week later she handed back everyone's graded paper, never asking me where my book report was. Maybe she was saving it for after class I thought but nothing happened after class. When I was on the bus going home, I felt like I had won. All that worry was for nothing, although I did have one small problem. Having seen the other book reports, I understood the assignment but still felt a little nervous that Miss. Shannon might ask the class to do another one. So from then on I decided to be a good girl and do my homework. Sure enough we were asked to do another book report. This one was an 'oral' book report. I asked what 'oral' meant. I was relieved because I had seen the movie 'Charlotte's Web', so many times and I didn't have to write about it, only talk about it and talking is one of my favorite things to do. To make a long story short, I got a B on it. I was starting to like learning a little more at this new school and happy that I was making new friends.

Because of my poor grades, my mom would make sure that I did my homework and made me read to her a chapter everyday until I finished the entire book. I hated reading out loud, but with her guidance I was turned on to books. I began reading more books on my own, and not just the ones I had to read in school. She also gave me exercises to do even when I didn't bring any work home. My grades started to improve as this went on.

Towards the end of my last year at St. Bonaventure elementary school; Father Paul would show up every Monday morning to take note of the students that were attending church on Sunday. That is if we were to be confirmed. Confirmation is a ceremony that took place in the church which was built next to our school. My mom and I stopped going but I attempted since it was a requirement. Actually there were a few of us that didn't get confirmed, it never matter to me as long as I was graduating. We had the option of going to a same sex or co-ed school. I was one of many who chose co-ed. Kelly and I would talk on the phone late at night about new teachers, boys, and sex. Everyone in our eighth grade class was excited about moving on to high school but not everyone would be choosing the same one, so it was a bitter-sweet evening for some of us. Nana and grandpa came to see me accept my diploma, and they took me out to dinner afterwards. Nana was proud and grandpa was preaching at me to straighten up and fly right, if I wanted to get in to college. My mom's only concern was that I graduate high school.

The first year of high school, I spent most of my time with friends. And I can truthfully say I was high on life. Grade nine was totally awesome! Every morning I woke up excited to see my friends at school; Kelly, Stacey, Lisa and me, the four of us always laughing at jokes. I didn't care about my grades because for the first time, school was fun. Especially since, it was an escape from the reality of being at home. I got along with everyone in school, except this one girl named Linda who decided I was her nemesis. I had no classes with her, nor did I know her well enough to be enemies with her in the first place, but for some reason she took a liking to me.

On my fifteenth birthday she wrote on my locker, **"Happy Birthday Bitch!"** using a thick black marker for all to see. How did she know it was my birthday? I was kind of flattered, even though she was calling me names. The only time I'd see her was when passing through the halls between classes. By then I had outgrown fighting, so I paid her no attention.

Going home after school was a downer because my mom became more withdrawn as time wore on. We hardly spent any time together like we used to. I'd ask her many times if she wanted to go out and do something together, have a little mother & daughter time. Sadly, she was never interested in doing anything other than sitting on the couch, smoking a cigarette and sipping apple juice. "What's that you're drinking?" I asked. "Apple juice" she replied. I went in the fridge to get some and found none there. Michael spent more and more time away on business. I enjoyed his absence, although, it was obvious he was having an affair.

My mom spent a week in the hospital, for reasons she never wanted to talk about and never wanted me to know. I called her everyday to find out what happened and see how she was. My mom was very withholding and insisted that I not come to see her. She told me not to worry and that she'll be home soon.

Her secretiveness, prompted me to follow her into their bathroom to see what she was doing. Along the counter was a line-up of pill bottles from one end to the next. I asked "What are all these pills for?" Embarrassed, she wasn't answering, instead behaving like a frightened child too afraid to speak. "What are all these pills for?" I pressed. Still no answer, I felt hopeless for her and I didn't know what to do or who to turn to. Wanting to get help I asked some of my peers about calling an abuse hotline or something. But I was told that to report any form of abuse had to be proven and that such accusations were considered a criminal offense. My mom begged me not to tell anyone when I threatened to get help and I threatened often. The more fearful she became of him the less fearful I became. I loved my mom and she was getting worse and no longer in control. I didn't know what to do. So I called my grandparents and explained what was happening. I knew my mom wouldn't approve so I called them without her knowing. They soon arrived kneeling next to her asking, "What's the matter?" My mom responded by crying uncontrollably. I left them, hoping her parents would help her and I prayed to God to give my mom the strength to leave him.

Two days after my fifteenth birthday, Kelly and I were giggling as we exchanged notes in English class. While Mr. Harris droned on about introductions, plots, characters, the climax, loose ends, all the necessary points of good story writing when our attention turned by a knock on the door. Everyone stopped talking, curiously looking toward the door at this rare intrusion, which usually meant someone was in trouble. Mr. Harris walked over and opened the door. One of the office secretaries stood in the doorway and spoke to him softly. Everyone remained silent, straining to hear. He motioned for her to come in and stepped back to give way. The woman barely entered the room when she asked for "Martika Pelletier." Wondering why I was being called, I got up and started to approach her. Then she told me to bring my coat. "Oooo..." my classmates teased. I ignored them as I grabbed my coat off the back of the chair then walked out of the classroom and into the hallway with the secretary. She told me to go to the Principal's office, "They will explain why they need to see you." she said. "Ok" I replied. The Principal's office was located in the O'Connor building only a short distance from the Lynch building, where our English class was held. It was a cold winter day. Watching my step as I walked over ice and snow, I tried to recall what I had done wrong and when nothing came to mind, I assumed I was being called about my reference card. Apparently, all catholic students at Senator O'Connor needed to be confirmed which I was not. In the O'Connor building the lady at the office window asked why I was sent. I told her it was about some mundane detail regarding my reference card. She told me that was not the Principal's concern and to go across the hallway and speak with a guidance counselor about the matter. I looked over at the guidance office and repeated. "But I was sent here, to the Principal's office." Confused, we looked blankly at each other. Mr. Gravelle, the Principal came out of another door, looked around, saw me and asked. "Are you Martika?" "Yes" I replied. "Did I say your name correctly?" he added. I nodded. "Come with me" he said. I gave the lady at the window a look then I followed him back through the door he came out of that was restricted to students. We traveled through a warm and narrow hallway passing two or three offices, until we reached the Vice Principals office. The Vice

Principal was an attractive full figured woman named Mrs. Glace. She was a kind and understanding lady who I was meeting for the first time. In her office sat Michael looking incredibly pale and nervous as though he was guilty of something. Surprised to see him I felt immediately tense by his presence, not wanting to hear anything unpleasant he had to say. Looking at me, I glared back at him, thinking. 'What did you do?' Mr. Gravelle closed the door and joined us. I was asked to sit down. Michael tried to speak. Mrs. Glace spoke first. "There's been an accident." she looked over at Michael to continue. "Your mother's been in an accident." He took a long pause, avoiding my eyes. "Well, how is she?" I asked impatiently. "She's dead." he said. I didn't want to believe what I heard. At first I thought I was the butt of a joke, I'm on the new 'Candid Camera' show. When there was no show host or camera crew running out to let me off the hook, I fell silent. Mrs. Glace and Mr. Gravelle offered their support and encouraged me to take all the time I needed. I was escorted back to class only to get my books. The jovial energy in the room ceased as I entered the room with a pale and stunned expression moving toward my desk in a dream like state. My escort summoned Mr. Harris outside of the classroom for the explanation of my dismissal. Everyone's eyes followed me, wondering what happened with perplexity written on their faces. As I picked up my books, Kelly asked, "What's wrong?" "I'll call you later." I mouthed, as no sound came out. I was joined by the police when I went back to the O'Connor building and they drove Michael and I home.

Once we were alone, he started to tell me how she died. He sat on the couch in the den while I remained standing. I waited, but my thoughts were, 'Whatever comes out of your mouth doesn't matter because you already killed her, long ago.' "She took her own life." he said. "What!" I gasped. "I'll kill her!" Not wanting to believe my mother would ever do such a thing. "How?" I commanded. Pointing to the window toward the front of our building, he said "She jumped off the bridge." "She jumped off the balcony?" I repeated confused. "No," he said and moved over to the window and pointed out, "That bridge over there, she was found in the park." I moved to the window and looked down. Across the street was a public high school, beside it was a ravine made into a provincial park and on the other side of the ravine were apartment buildings. The bridge, running east and west could be seen clearly from where we stood. I started to interrogate him. "Why do you think she did it?" "When did she do it?" "Who found her?" and "Where were you?" Michael tried to answer as best he could then he began crying. "I wish I could be as strong as you." "I have to be." I replied without knowing why I was saying what I was saying, and I stormed off into my room while he began calling family and friends. "Marilyn's gone" he wept.

A couple days later, I woke up from a deep sleep. My bedroom door was open and I could see my mom and Michael's room door was ajar. Getting out of bed, I went into their room and saw my mom sleeping in the bed alone. Relieved to see her there, now believing it was all just a bad dream. I knelt by her side waking her gently saying, "Mom, mom, where have you been? You have been gone for two months. Why did you leave me? Why didn't you tell me you were going?" Half asleep she said that she had to get away, "I just had to get away." she muttered. I jolted up and looked around. My bedroom door was open, their bedroom door was closed. My first reaction was to see if she was really there but I knew she was not. It was a wishful dream. The nightmare I was living was a painful reality. Feeling distraught about the situation the dream made me realize that, God had answered my prayer. It turns out she did receive the strength to leave him after all.

Michael was rarely home during the time off I took from school. I spent much time alone with my thoughts wandering around the living room; then came to the conclusion that I wanted to be with her. I didn't see any point in living without her. She was my nurturer, my teacher and my best friend; My everything. All that I had ever known, all that she has taught me and all the love I'd felt; came from her. I had nothing, I felt nothing and was nothing; A voided life, an empty corpse, the walking dead. Being without her caused such tremendous grief, that the sorrow began eating away at me, creating a hole at the pit of my soul. A pain I could no longer bear, I decided right then and there to join her. Wherever she was had to be better than this and I had no desire to be left with my stepfather, who I detested enough, to gladly have seen him killed instead. I drifted over to the window, slid it open all the way and looked down. Then I climbed onto the ledge. There was no screen and my small body stood in the frame. All it would have taken is one step and down I would go, a twenty story fall away, to be with her again. I proceeded. From out of nowhere a force of some kind, knocked me back into the living room and a wave of peace I never felt before invoked an awareness. *"You are not meant to follow and therefore must live on."* A voice said.

The next day, I decided to return to school only because being alone didn't make me feel better. Being at school didn't make me feel any better either. I went from being happy and enthusiastic to angry and sad. Many rumors were floating around about my mom's death. The rumors spread so quickly from my perception because of having friends in four other high schools, all calling me on the phone to talk about it. "It was on the news", an acquaintance told me. Some students heard that she was raped then killed, while other stories were that she killed herself because her daughter was black. To make matters worse, Linda was still tormenting me. I saw her standing across the crowded hallway ridiculing me. The anger inside me was mounting and all the pain and frustration were fully charged. I was about to give Linda the beating of a lifetime, when another wave of peace swept over me, taking away all my negative feelings. I loved the harmonious feelings but was a little annoyed that I wasn't able to fight her.

I was in a funk and I couldn't relate with my friends anymore, so I turned to music and music became my friend and only comfort. Songs such as *Blasphemous Rumors* by

Depeche Mode were among my favorite. "…I don't want to start any blasphemous rumors but I think that God's got a sick sense of humor and when I die, I expect to find him laughing."

I never did see her body after she died. It would have interested me to see if there were any additional cuts or bruises on her before she was cremated which was her final wish. I blamed Michael and the prescribed drugs she was taking that prompted her to end her life. Her mind wasn't right and I had my doubts about what had really happened that night. Since the police never questioned me, they might have questioned Michael but who knows what really happened once they found her. The cause of death was suicide, end of story. Her memorial was held at our church, St. John XXIII. The place was packed with many people that I hadn't seen in some time. I sat there still believing that it was all an elaborate joke. None of this was real, it wasn't true. I convinced myself that she staged her own death just to get away from him. Thinking to myself, 'I will wake up from this nightmare, she will reappear and we will be happy again.'

At the end of the school year, my final report card showed a drastic decline in marks and was viewed by my stepfather, who sat me down at the dining room table and asked why my grades were so poor. Then he told me I needed to show more improvement. I just looked at him blankly, but what I really wanted to say was, 'Are you for real? My mom just died you asshole. How on earth could I concentrate on school?' But I refrained because I did not want another unjust beating. If things weren't bad enough, questions began to arise from family members and close friends implying that he murdered my mom, and made it look like a suicide. Those were the testimonies of the select few who knew of his abusive behavior. I prayed to God to give me strength not to kill him myself. I never in my life thought about killing another human being until he came along. I thought about hiring someone to take him out, or poisoning his food or using a blunt object on him while he slept so that he may never wake up, ever again.

They eventually winterized their cottage because they planned on living there all year round, once they both retired. Uncle Don and Aunt Maureen lived a short distance from their place. The main street consisted of a bank, a variety store, a pharmacy, a bakery, a sporting goods store, a grocery store and a two storey house made into the town hall called the Alcona Business Center. Driving down the main strip, Nana used to say, "We're approaching downtown Alcona, don't blink or you'll miss it." In the summer I'd stay for a week or so. It was a popular place to be, bustling with city dwellers kicking back and enjoying the lake but as the seasons changed it became considerably quiet especially in the winter months. There weren't any high schools, only one elementary school. All the teenagers had to take school buses into Barrie. Barrie is a small city that has four public high schools and one catholic high school, named St. Joseph that my grandparents encouraged my aunt and uncle to enroll me in. Uncle Don and Aunt Maureen made me feel right at home. They were kind to take me in and I felt deeply grateful, though I might not have shown it. Aunt Maureen gave me a diary to write in. She said it would help me deal with my feelings. I wrote in it nearly every day. They also suggested that I get counseling, to discuss my mom's death and to talk about anything else that was concerning me.

It wasn't hard for me to make new friends but none of them lived in Alcona. Most of them stayed in Barrie which was a thirty minute drive. Since there was no public bus service, I spent the majority of my time at home without anyone my age to hang out with. I did happen to find out, that the kids my age in Alcona went to a public school called Innisdale. I decided to switch schools after I was through with grade ten. My grandparents weren't thrilled with the idea of my leaving the catholic school and even more disappointed when I told them I didn't want to go to church anymore. Because they were making it a habit of picking me up every Sunday morning, assuming I still went to church.

St. Joseph High School reminded me of the movie called 'Revenge of the Nerds' mostly because many of them went there. Also I didn't agree with their teaching when it came to religion. I found it confusing and conflicting. I was taught that God is all loving and all forgiving however there were some exceptions to this. For example, if you take the lord's name in vain you go to hell or if you take your own life you go to hell as well. I never believed for one second, my mom went to hell because she committed suicide. I didn't think God would ever do that to someone who loves him/her so much and just needed to get away from a terrible relationship. Surely God could make an exception or two. I had my very own understanding of who I thought God was. From then on, I decided not to follow the catholic faith and instead follow what was truly in my heart.

During that same year, I had to do a presentation for health class, a five minute speech on the topic of choice. Thinking,... should I discuss boys, relationships, nature, science or health since it was a health class. I went through many subjects, but nothing fit. I couldn't think of anything cool to talk about but I knew once I had a topic, I would have no problem writing about it. The assignment was based on communication, (verbal and non-verbal) and so we were being assessed on our body language as we read our speeches. How nerve racking, especially for shy teenagers. We had two weeks to do the assignment, the last week being March break. Meaning I gave myself one week to write it since I had plans to visit my friends in Toronto. Preoccupied with March break madness, I didn't do the assignment. In fact, I don't recall any of us doing the assignment. On the first day back to school, I was feeling a little anxious about being unprepared. I walked into class to take my seat and amazingly there was a substitute teacher standing in front of the room ready to introduce herself. What a relief. God is good. Once we were all seated she got right to it. "Mrs. Humphries tells me you have a speech assignment due today?" Some students nodded in agreement. "Well, she continued, who's ready to present?" No one raised their hand. Then she asked "By a show of hands, who completed the assignment?" No one raised their hand. She excused us but warned Mrs. Humphries would be back tomorrow and to have our speeches ready. That night I knew I had to decide on a topic but all I kept thinking about was all the fun I had on the March break, I really had a great time. I thought maybe I should write about that but then changed my mind because it sounded so elementary as I was in High School and the students would surely laugh at me. Then my inner voice said, "It will be funny and therefore cool and besides you have no other ideas and you are out of time." I couldn't argue with that logic, so I wrote a couple of pages about my week, Monday through Friday but I didn't quite make it to Friday. I fell asleep, it was late. The very next day I tried to finish my speech on the school bus and in math class before health class but I somehow failed. So I sat in health class with a half written speech. Needless to say I was not prepared. Mrs. Humphries hearing of our neglectfulness began. "You've all had ample time to complete the assignment.

Who would like to go first?" No one raised their hand. "I see, we will have a draw to see who goes first." she addressed. We all picked a number out of a cup. Guess which number I got? That's right, number one. I was panicking. The girl who was sitting next to me asked discreetly, "What number did you get?" "One," I told her. "Do you mind switching with me? I want to get mine over with." she said. I gratefully exchanged numbers with her. Her number was ten. See how good god is. I was able to continue writing my speech while the others read theirs.

Mrs. Humphries asked the class to help her observe the presenter's every movement. After each speech, we discussed the body language. Noting, hand movements, and the nervous shifting from side to side. Everyone was nervous. Some stood there with their papers in front of their faces reading their boring speeches not making any eye contact. Being criticized was making the ordeal even more painful for whoever was up next because the topic didn't matter only the body language. My number was slowly creeping up, seven, eight, then nine. I was almost done writing my speech. "Who's next, where's number ten?" Mrs. Humphries asked looking around the room. "Me." I said and got up to go to the front of the class, back straight, with paper in hand, read. "What I did on the March break." Everyone burst out laughing, including Mrs. Humphries. I giggled nervously, hiding behind my paper briefly before continuing. I was really trying to give a serious speech here. I started to relax as the outburst broke the tension. I continued speaking and the class continued laughing. I didn't care if they were laughing with me or at me, making more movements than anyone else. I felt so relieved after. I thought I was going to crash and burn but instead I came out on top giving the last presentation of the day, beginning with a laughing ovation. I was on a high when it was over and discovered that making people laugh really does feel good.

Once I switched schools things really started to happen for me. I had friends to hang out with; Carrie, Dori, Lucy and Shelly. All living in close proximity to me. Innisdale was all that I imagined a fully equipped facility to be. The school was a lot bigger than St. Joes and offered more courses. Most of the school was carpeted an orange, reddish color, while the lockers were painted blue, green, and orange. Our school colors were blue and orange. Those of us that came by school bus arrived early so we sat in the halls until classes started. Life was fun again. It was my friends that I would look forward to seeing every day, school itself, never really interested me much. Although Mr. Bell's creative writing course was one of my favorite classes. He was an easy going, laid back kind of guy. His creative writing motto or definition was to write the way you feel. Be creative. There was no right or wrong way to do it. I loved it because there were no rules to this kind of homework. He would also let us have free reign during class time but profanity was not allowed. Using swear words got you kicked out of the class and then you had to sit in the hall for the duration of the period. Since we all thought Mr. Bell was the coolest, we respected his discipline.

One morning we had an assembly in the auditorium, I think it was about aids or something. It took all of the first period before the assembly was over and it was time for second period classes to begin. Carrie and I were laughing about the presentation on our way to creative writing. She was mocking the speaker and exaggerating on how having sex with a green monkey gave you aids. Carrie was always talking bullshit to me and as we walked in the room I said, "Get the fuck out!" Suddenly realizing where I was, I looked over at Mr. Bell, who was sitting at his desk in front of the room, looked at me and I said, "I know, wait outside." I hated having to sit in the hall by myself, but all was not lost. I kept getting visitors. Lucy had a spare, "Wha cha doin out here?" she asked as she sat next to me. "I got kicked out for swearing." "Well I'll keep you company for a while then I gotta go." We chatted for a bit then she took off. A guy going to the washroom passed by, while coming back he asked what crime I committed. Before I could tell him, he guessed, "Swearing in Mr. Bell's class right?" A few more students saw me sitting by the door and asked what happened and that sparked a whole conversation. When one had to go back to class, someone came out of another, just to use the bathroom or whatever. They came in increments. The whole hour and fifteen minutes went like that. Classes ended and everyone filed out of the rooms. I stood watching everyone leave, waiting for Mr. Bell to make his appearance. Before he could speak I babbled, "I know I'm not suppose to swear in class, I'm sorry I promise it won't happen again." He said "Ok. Good." and said nothing more. I walked away feeling that that punishment was no punishment at all, so I turned around and said, "By the way, thanks for the spare." Smiling, he shook his head and walked back into the classroom.

My friends and I planned a camping trip at the Four Seasons campground, north of Orillia on the May Victoria long weekend also known as the May two-four weekend. We were all excited about going, the news said it would rain all weekend both TV and radio stations said so. We ignored the forecast and focused on having fun in the sun and left Friday morning, driving in the rain for a couple of hours. When we reached our reserved campsite it continued to rain while we set up our tents. Everyone but Shelly helped, she sat in the car so her teased hair wouldn't get wet. About the time we were done setting the tents up and got the blue tarp over the picnic table, the rain stopped and the sun came out. Everyone started to celebrate. We ate hamburgers, hotdogs and drank wild berry coolers then went around the camp to tour the washrooms, showers and fenced in outdoor pool. There was even a dirt pit for dirt bikes. Although some four by four vehicles ventured in making it a fun pit and we found ourselves in the bed of a pickup truck that got stuck on a steep slope. The pit was muddy on account of the rain and the truck felt like it was about to turn over on its back, with us in it. We were scared sober. Luckily two guys in a jeep drove around to ask if we wanted to come out. "That's not safe; you girls better come with us." The driver said. They could see that the driver of the truck was completely drunk as were most of the drivers in the pit. We were more than glad to get out of there. Then we went back to our campsite and ate potato chips and drank some more.

That first night; me, Carrie, Dori, Lucy and Shelly decided to go for a walk to check out the guys, and made up a routine spot check, calling it the pecker patrol. "We're the pecker patrol so we'll need to see your peckers." We explained as we approached them in the dark with our flashlights.

The night after we went to a party on the other side of the campground in an open field where many were gathered listening to rock music, dancing, drinking and smoking around a bonfire. Carrie and Dori were returning from the washrooms, laughing at what they had witnessed. "What's so funny?" I asked. "Some guy was screwing his girlfriend on the side of the road and a car drove over his legs, all you could hear was a crack, then 'Argh,' another crack, then 'Argh!'" They continued laughing, I didn't believe them. Carrie was always bullshitting. "Where?"

I asked. "Right over there!" They pointed and howled. Beyond the open field was a narrow dirt road in a wooded area. I questioned further. "But how?" "The woman was lying on her back with her legs up in the air and the guy was on top with his legs on the ground, the driver didn't see them." They laughed. They kept on laughing; it was the funniest thing they'd ever seen. I still didn't believe them.

The next morning I crawled out of the tent and went to the washroom. The place was quiet; everyone was still out from the night before. I passed one campsite where a man was sleeping, sitting upright in his lawn chair, head back, mouth wide open still holding a beer can in one hand and a burnt down cigarette in the other. Once everyone woke up, we ended up in the pool after we ate breakfast. A red truck drove up alongside the pool. The driver opened his door, got out and clung to the fence with his hands, using his arms to hold himself up. I went over to him, "What happened to you?" Still drunk he replied, "I was making love to my girlfriend on the side of the road and my legs got run over." "You'd better go to the hospital". I interjected. "Oh, I'll be alright". He slurred, in his smashed state. I looked over at Carrie. "I told you", she said.

On our last night at Four Seasons, many of us crammed onto a wide flat bed truck and drove around the campsites. Everyone singing "Na, na, na, na, - na, na, na, na, hey, hey, hey, goodbye."

The summer that followed was warmer than usual. Nana suffered from asthma and was having trouble with the heat. Grandpa was about to install an air conditioner, when she had an asthma attack that left her in the hospital. The doctor was not hopeful because she wasn't breathing on her own. They put her on a respirator, she died two days later. Grandpa was devastated of her passing. He was no longer the authoritative type, giving plenty of disciplinary verbiage every time we'd visit. "You'd better pull up your socks and buckle down." No, he was not the same man. He was quite different. My grandparents were very social and always doing things together, such as playing golf, cards and traveling to places. No longer having the zest for life, grandpa gave up, developing one disease after the next. First he had cataracts, then his bladder stopped working and his liver started to fail. He spent most of his time with us and we took care of him.

The last year of high school flew by so fast, mainly because we were having so much fun being seniors. I passed all my classes, graduated in the spring of '88 and moved back to Toronto. I stayed with friends and got a job working as an usher at a theatre downtown in the evenings and worked at a survey company during the day. Grandpa phoned, wanting to meet with me in the city for lunch. He sat me down and told me that he didn't have much time left. His acceptance speech went, "I've lived a good full life." Then he looked at me with stern eyes and began, "I feel sorry for you," he said. "Losing your mother, grandmother and now me, well kiddo, that's life. You'll be alright, but be careful of the friends you're staying with, I don't trust them."

He died two years after her. I inherited a large sum of money because of their deaths, though some would call it was a blessing, I didn't because it didn't bring anyone back. It's not the same as winning a lottery. Their lives were replaced with money, someone had to die in order to receive it. Although I felt relieved and comforted that grandpa was home and with nana again, I deeply missed them.

I took grandpa's advice and got my own place and left the theatre after receiving a promotion from the survey company.

In August 1990, I was busy at work keeping up with other departments, getting data out before the deadline, when I got a call from my cousin Mark. Uncle Don had been in a car accident. "How is he?" I asked. "Not good." Mark said, holding back his emotion, then gave me the name of the hospital they were at. A sudden wave of disbelief came over me and I didn't want the worst to happen. I could hear it in his voice that it wasn't good. I said that I was on my way and asked the name of the hospital again. After I hung up the phone, I explained to my supervisor why I had to leave. She gave her support while my co-workers looked on with concern. "Are you ok to drive?" a co-worker asked. "Yeah" I said. But I wasn't. I forgot the name of the hospital again and then remembered it was Sunnybrook after I calmed myself for a moment. Once I arrived, the nurses at admitting didn't have any information regarding my uncle. I went from one department to the next asking of his whereabouts. Getting a little frustrated, I finally found Mark and Aunt Maureen. Uncle Don was in the intensive care unit all bandaged up and hooked up to machines. The doctor said there was extensive brain damage if he did manage to pull through he would be a vegetable. None of us wanted that for him. He died twenty four hours later.

The accident happened on highway 400 when a transport truck coming from the opposite direction, entered the oncoming traffic causing a fatal multi-collision, killing him, among others. The highway was closed off for awhile and my uncle was air lifted to the hospital. I was up early and on my way to the hospital when they told me of his passing. We talked about going home to make the necessary funeral arrangements. Mark rode with me. I was nervous about driving for some reason. We were traveling along highway 401 approaching the 400 when a rusty old brown car was about to collide into me from the left. I honked and stared at the driver, wanting him to be aware that I was there. I sped up and he moved behind me. With that near miss out of the way I relaxed, slowly merging over to the right hand side of the four lane highway as the 400 north exit was approaching. There was a transport truck to my right, driving by it was a bang, and we began to spin. I tried to steer but the car was moving out of my control. It reminded me of being in a bumper car turning the wheel all the way and bang, I hit someone. Another bang I'd been hit, still spinning fast and in slow motion until the car came to a full stop. Silence consumed us.

We had done a complete 360 degree turn and ended up on the far left hand side of the four lane highway. "Are you alright? Are you alright?" I asked excitedly. "Yea, are you?" Mark answered. "Yea" I said. "What do I do now?" "Pull over to the side" he said. I eased the car onto the shoulder and put the hazard lights on. We got out of the car to survey the damage. There were a couple of minor dents with the back right wheel dramatically bent inward. Mark picked up a bolt off the ground that looked like it had been there for years and said, "Does this belong to you?" We burst out laughing, then observed that the traffic had come to a halt and laughed some more. "We stopped traffic." Mark said happily. The laughter tapered off as we noticed two tow truck drivers on the other side of the meridian. "Did you see the accident?" I addressed. They just stared at us. I wondered what the matter was, but I supposed they don't see many people laughing after an accident. We waited for the police to arrive and called home. Aunt Maureen's friend answered. She was already at the house preparing for all of us to come home from the hospital. When I told her why we were running behind, she promised not to tell my aunt.

We knew Aunt Maureen wouldn't be able to handle any more bad news. Mark and I showed up a few hours later as if nothing happened.

I was allotted a few days off work to be with my family, wondering the whole time why God took Uncle Don. About a week later I saw him in a dream. He was happy and playing with others. I woke up the next morning feeling at peace.

With most of my immediate family gone, I decided to find my father. I was thirteen the last time I had seen him when he showed up at our apartment unannounced. My mom opened the door and almost fainted at the sight of him standing there. It was evident to me that she still had feelings for him. Michael was in their room sleeping after returning from a long business trip. My father said he recently moved to Toronto, and was living with his new wife, and gave a brief summary of what he had been up too. He offered to take me out for lunch. We waited in the lobby for a cab to take us over to the Don

Mills shopping center. Every time I looked at him, he was staring at me. He commented on how beautiful I had become. His daunting over me made me feel a little uneasy, but loved. We ate lunch in a restaurant and chatted. I felt a little awkward. I didn't know him well and wasn't sure how to address him; Dad or Deacon. Feeling somewhat abandoned by him over the years, I tried not to address him at all and although our visit was pleasant, it was brief.

Many years had gone by since then and it was May 1993. I thought I had a serious case of death anxiety. First my mom died, two years later my nana, my grandpa followed two years after her and a year later Uncle Don. Just as I was getting over one death; there was another funeral to go to. Thoughts of my father dying from aids crossed my mind and I was on fire to find him. I had a feeling that his marriage with his latest wife had ended. My father loved women and was often in and out of relationships. I figured he was probably living back in the Bahamas, since he detested the cold. I didn't think it would be hard to find him. The Bahamas is very small in comparison to Canada. Everyone practically knows one another. I went to the Toronto Reference Library, where they have international telephone books. Luckily they had The Bahamas. The phone book wasn't current but that didn't matter. I photocopied all the Whyllys on the page, called some when I got home with no luck, but a few days later I contacted a cousin named Desmond.

I introduced myself and said, "I'm looking for Deacon Whylly. I'm his daughter, the one in Canada." "Oh, you're in Canada." Desmond said sounding a little surprised. He told me he didn't know where my father was but would pass the message on that I was looking for him and would call with any information.

Days turned into weeks and weeks turned into months and I was still waiting to hear back from Desmond. I wanted to hear something, anything, thinking perhaps I'm just over reacting. Everything will be fine. I'll find him and everything will be ok. He's not going to die from aids or anything. I'm just experiencing a case of death anxiety.

Desmond called two months later saying they found my father, but he died two days ago. I didn't know whether to laugh or cry. "Two days ago! Two days ago? How did he die?" "Cancer." Desmond said.

A few days later after returning home from work, I received a message from a woman in the Bahamas. Her name was Anita, and she left a number. I called back and spoke with her. I asked again how he died. Prostate cancer she told me. "Are you a friend or relative of his?" I went on. "I'm ya sista!" Anita informed as if I should have known this already. Immediately tears swelled in my eyes as she went on to say that I have, including herself, four older sisters; Serena, the eldest, Anita then Corrina and Pearly. Serena and Anita have the same mother and was our father's first wife. Serena is married with four daughters and Anita has a daughter. They live in Florida while Corrina and Pearly live in Texas and have the same mother. Corrina has a daughter and Pearly has a son and daughter. I was overwhelmed. She asked if I would be coming to the funeral. I said I wanted too but wasn't able. She understood, and then admitted that it was aids he died from. We agreed to keep in touch now that we found each other and ended the conversation on that note.

"God doesn't take away without giving back." was whispered in my ear as I hung up the phone.

Part Two

The plane was descending on the runway and my heart was beating fast. As soon as it landed and docked at Miami's International Airport, a flight attendant announced over the speaker, "Martika Whylly your party will meet you at the front gate." Excited with anticipation, I grabbed my bag from the over head compartment and imagined what my sister looked like. Serena and I had corresponded on the phone and agreed to meet on the Canadian Thanksgiving weekend. I sent a recent photo, so she would know what I looked like and was hoping to meet Anita as well but she was in Nassau.

A stream of hot air blew over my face as I exited the plane and walked through a humid tunnel. I started to turn the corner with the flow of passengers heading for the baggage and claims area when I saw an expressionless couple off to my right standing alone. I did a double take and started towards them. "Serena?" "Yea," she said simply, and then introduced me to my brother in-law Smiley. "I almost passed you. You know what I look like, why didn't you say something?" I asked. "I wanted to see if you recognize family. You should know your own blood," she answered.

I couldn't believe it, here I was meeting family for the first time, and this woman was testing me. I had seen many families reunite on various talk shows and it was always a joyful and tearful reunion. This however was somewhat different, no hugs or kisses. Maybe it was because there was no audience or camera crew around.

On the ride back to their house, my sister and I got better acquainted. "I've been looking for you on Oprah," Serena mentioned. "Really?" I said. "It's funny you would say that, because I was thinking about contacting the Oprah show to find our father, when they were looking for guests wanting to find long lost relatives. But then again, the thought of millions of people watching, made me change my mind. Anyway, I knew I would find you just the same." I beamed. When we reached their house, I met all four of my adorable nieces. The talkative one asked her mom, "This your sister? How come we never see her?" Serena explained that I live in Canada and didn't know them until now. After settling in, we looked through the photo album I brought with me. Serena was able to identify the people my mom vaguely spoke about. "That's me, with you and your mom." she pointed. "An me and Anita." We chatted about the pictures and our father some. Then she showed me a few of his funeral photos. She'd been wondering if she would ever see me again, being eleven years older than me. "I used to baby sit you." she informed. I was too young to remember and confessed that my mom was very secretive and said little about life in the Bahamas.

"Yea, we finally found this crazy girl," Serena grinned on the phone to Pearly in Texas. Listening in, I lounged on her bed with my nieces gathered around. "All us Whylly girls should get togetha for Christmas so save money and book time now," she went on. It had been a while since Serena had seen Pearly or Corrina and thought Christmas would be a fine time to get together. I was so excited; meeting more siblings was a dream come true.

A couple of months later I went back to visit Serena and them. It felt weird spending Christmas away from the snow. Serena told me Anita would already be at their house by the time I got there.

When I arrived in Florida, the sun welcomed me with its warmth, and the palm trees waved to me in the light breeze as I waited outside the terminal for them to pick me up. I recognized Serena's daughter in the car that was slowly approaching. She recognized me too. I didn't recognize the woman driver and assumed it was Anita. She pulled over and we smiled at each other. Then she got out and greeted me with a hug saying "I kept forgetting just because we've been talking on the phone doesn't mean we know what the other looks like, that's why Rudy came." "That's good." I answered. "But I sent Serena a photo, didn't you see it?" "Naw." she said. On the way to the house we discussed whether Corrina and Pearly were coming.

We were happily greeted by our nieces as we opened the front door and there in the living room next to the window was a large beautifully decorated Christmas tree. In the background was the faint sound of the TV, barely audible above the noise made by our holiday cheer. Serena told me to put my things in Rudy's room as Anita was staying in the talkative one's room.

While the children were in the family room watching TV, the three of us sat at the kitchen table, talking and getting to know one another. As they spoke, I noticed the American accent fade and more Bahamian dialect could be heard and my mind started to drift. At one point in the conversation Serena stopped talking and looked at me then looked at Anita and said "She don't understand us." They both laughed. I smiled meekly because she was right, I didn't understand. Even though I grew up in a multi-cultural environment most of my life, and heard many dialects, I didn't know any Bahamians.

The day before Christmas, we were in the kitchen preparing the turkey and all the fixin's when I asked. "So tell me more about our father. What was it like growing up with him?" They told me about his life and stories of their childhood. I told them. "He came to me in a dream. He was floating towards me through a cloud and his arms were stretched out to embrace me."

Serena said our father came to her in a dream as well, wearing a white suit, and sitting on her bed telling her, "Everything will be ok, everything will be alright," with his hand pressed on her shoulder. I thought it was amazing that we were seeing him in our dreams. "Isn't it great that he's communicating with us?" I said to them. "Yea, but while he up there with God, he could at least give us the winning lotto numbers, soes we don't have to worry." Serena laughed.

At night my nieces and I went for a walk around the neighbourhood to look at all the decorative and brightly lit homes. One house had a gigantic white sheet on their front lawn. I was touched because I missed the snow. Also was a little disappointed that Corrina and Pearly were no shows. Serena, Anita, and I called Pearly and Corrina to cuss them out. "You spose ta be here wit us," Serena griped. "Anita an Martika here. Why you couldn't be here, and all us Whylly girls be togetha. You said you was coming, ya'll lying deep front heiffas." She snickered then asked if "Everyone ok?" before passing the phone onto us. Anita and I took turns talking to them and we wished everyone a Merry Christmas and said 'I love you,' before ending the exchange.

The following year Serena tried getting the Whylly sisters together on the American Thanksgiving weekend. I attended and Pearly came with her two children but Corrina and Anita couldn't make it. I'll never forget the way Serena introduced me to Pearly. I followed Serena into the family room where Pearly was waiting. When I heard her say jokingly, "See ya sista, she on crack!" Gazing upon Pearly, all I could do was smile, thinking 'I hope she knows Serena's bullshittin. I've never done crack in my life.' Noticing the expression on my face, Serena added "All us Whylly girls are wild and crazy. Didn't you know that?" I simply blushed.

****

When I wasn't traveling to the United States (averaging once a year) I was at work or with friends or with my boyfriend and visiting family or at the library. The library was where I went to reassess my thoughts. Daydreaming was my favorite thing to do while I was there. I read books on the meaning of life, mainly on death and dying because I wanted to understand the whole process. Also studying books on philosophy and psychology, but mostly, I wanted to know God. I'd read a couple of pages of 'Conversations with God' by Neale Donald Walsch and my thoughts would wander off into forever. The library became a place of meditation, my sanctuary. Reading books felt like eating a succulent meal; tasting concepts, chewing on ideas, rolling my tongue over the words and caressing each phrase before I swallowed. My hunger for knowledge led me to 'The Magic of Believing' by Claude Bristol, 'Grow Rich! With Peace of Mind' by Napoleon Hill and inspirational books by Og Mandino, one of my all-time favourite authors. Their words would carry me far away and before I knew it, I'd be in another dimension. Suddenly, I'd snap out of tranquility, realize the time and head back to reality.

Serena called to tell me Anita was getting married to Basil on April 6, 1996. I took a couple weeks off work and went to Florida for their wedding. Serena and Smiley's house was full of relatives. I was always meeting more family members; Serena's Ma and Smiley's Ma or another sister of my sister's or my brother-in-law's sister's daughter or cousin and their children. Getting ready for the big day, folks were in and out the house running errands such as going to the store or to the hotel or the airport to pick up more relatives. It was a constant show. Serena and Smiley had automatic talking doors installed in their home, so every time the front door opened, the door said "front door," while the back door said, "back door" when it opened. Every few minutes or so someone would be coming in or going out, the doors chattered all day, "front door, back door, back door, front door." By late afternoon, the doors spoke less. Most of the children were inside watching TV while the adults and adolescences mingled in small groups out front. I went to lie down in my niece's room, with the warmth of the sun pouring in, and the love of kin put me at ease and I fell into a blissful sleep.

I was jarred out of a pleasant dream by some commotion coming from outside. When I woke up, I tried to recapture the dream, but all I could remember was that it felt really good. Rubbing my eyes, I stumbled over to open the door and the door said, "front door" and drowsily walked outside. Everyone's attention was turned at Keisha who was cussing and carrying on. Keisha was a close friend who lived next door. I lagged passed my sisters who were sitting on the porch, and stood in the center of the yard watching. Keisha spotted me and directed her anger my way saying, "And you...!" I barely knew her and didn't know what the fuss was. Before I could say anything, she was coming at me. She was taller than me, had an athletic body and was going to attack. I was in no mood to fight, so I closed my eyes and braced myself for the ass whipping I was about to receive. She got two feet from me then stopped, gripped her forehead and said, "I have a sharp pain in my head." Bowing back and forth in agony, repeated, "I have a sharp pain in my head." I watched in amazement. Here I was about to get a serious beat down for no reason and a miracle occurred. Out of nowhere I declared, "That's right! You don't want to mess with me cuz there's an army behind me and you can't see them cuz they're Angels!" Keisha's cousin, who was sitting on the car next to her, got scared and moved further away saying, "You know when someone talks like that they mean it." Keisha didn't respond she stayed bowing and holding her head in agony. No one else spoke. I marched back into the house and into my niece's room, lied on the bed, but could not fall asleep.

****

When the year 2000 approached many feared the end was near, as the media pumped terror into the minds of the people. There was much hearsay about a massive power outage or technical/computer crash that was supposed to affect everyone. Some were stalking up on can goods, water and other provisions, while others were preparing for the worst by collecting weapons and ammunition. For me the year 2000 only meant that I was turning thirty. What is a number anyway? It's just a number; Thirty, two thousand, two thousand and thirty, so instead of following the paranoia, I made up my mind to reflect upon my life and what I truly wanted out of it.

After much meditation on the matter, I came to the conclusion that I wanted to know my father. But he was already home with God. How was I going to get to know someone who has long gone? Then the answer came, "If you want to know me go to the Bahamas and get to know your family." I could feel his presence. "Knowing them is, knowing me."

In the spring of 2001 I left my job, my boyfriend and planned a trip to the Bahamas. I decided if I liked it and was able to work, then maybe I'll become a permanent resident, since I have both Bahamian and Canadian status. Making the necessary arrangements I sold furniture, gave away clothes and other items I would not need. When I told Serena of my plans she wanted me to stay with her and live and work in Florida. But my mind was firmly made up to go to the Bahamas. "You have family in Florida too." she reminded. We compromised and I decided to drive to Florida keeping my car so I could get around while I stayed with her a short time before moving to Nassau.

When I drove up to the Canadian - U.S. border, the guard at the American customs asked. "Where are you going?" "Florida." I said. "How long are you staying in Florida?" he questioned. "Two weeks." I replied. I was pulled aside, searched and denied entry because I had too much stuff and it looked like I was moving and planning to stay in the United States. I drove away feeling defeated but my willpower remained strong. A week later I tried again after lightening my load. Again American customs pulled me aside. "Where are you going?" the agent behind the counter asked. "Florida" I responded. "Why are you going to Florida?" he interrogated. I gave him the most determined look and said "To be with my sister and her four kids." I continued staring at him with unwavering faith that I must see my family. He stared back at me, and my soul spoke to his. After reviewing my papers, I was granted entry.

On the drive down I called from a pay phone early in the morning on day two to let Serena know I was on my way. For some reason she didn't believe I was coming. I irrevocably said "I'm in North Carolina! It'll probably take me another twelve hours or so. I don't know what time I'll be there but you better be up!"

When I finally arrived in Florida it was well past 11pm. I was so happy that I remembered all the road signs every time I visited. I was able to find their place no problem. When I got to the house, Serena looked out her bedroom window and opened the front door, greeted me with a hug then went back to bed.

Sitting on Rudy's bed I told my nieces of my road travels while I ate salad in a takeout container from Wendy's. "You drove all the way from Canada all by yourself?" the talkative one asked. "Yep and now my butt's numb" I giggled.

It was great spending time with them. Plus it took no time for Serena to hook me up with some single men she knew. I hated being set up, "This my sister. She's thirty one and staying with me," she'd say to them. I loved that she was trying to help but men were the farthest from my mind at the time. Somehow I couldn't get away from her saying "Maybe if you met someone who has somethin and wants somethin outta life you could get married and be close ta us." She was always trying to get me to stay, at the same time school me on men. I did go on some dates but wasn't really into any of them. On the other hand, I liked spending time with Bryon. I met him at Denny's one night while out with my nieces.

The first time Bryon came by to pick me up, he met my sister. Serena didn't seem to mind him. She was my mother and father. As we were leaving I heard, "Be home before midnight, a lady doesn't stay out past that," she'd sermon. I wanted to remind her I was grown but decided not to. The funny thing about it was that, at thirty one I had curfew.

Bryon didn't mind that she was strict. He was cool about it. "That's her way of showing her love for you." he said. "Yea, I know." I sighed.

We would go out for dinner and talk about life. I didn't always come home before twelve. My sister wouldn't mention it, but my niece made sure to ask while we ate breakfast. "How come you came home at two? You were supposed to be home at ten." The talkative one said.

"Was I supposed to be home at ten? My bad, I must've got my T's mixed up, two, ten, two to ten, ten to two. It's real confusing." I teased smiling at her.

When September came around I was ready to move on. Serena and I had been talking about where I would stay in Nassau. She suggested that I contact our cousin and find out about available jobs.

The morning after, the talkative one woke me up and told me to come in her parents' room. "Ma's on the phone." she said. Serena was calling from work. I slowly got out of bed and followed wondering what this crazy lady wanted so early in the morning. Entering their room the TV was on, showing a picture of the twin towers. One was on fire and a plane crashed into the other. I wondered what kind of show this was. I got on the phone. "You seeing this?" she said. "Yea," I replied, and then I passed the phone back to my niece.

I went back into Rudy's room, turned on the TV and continued watching the buildings burn. News reports were already pointing the blame on terrorism. I knew who was behind it but who would believe me?

One night Byron and I were out and I tried to explain to him that Bush was behind the attacks of the world trade center. He argued, "There's no way he could've done it. The man cried standing at ground zero." "He's a good actor." I explained. "Remember the movie The Princess Bride'? I continued without waiting for a response. "It's a fairy tale about true love. Wesley and Buttercup were in love. Whereas Prince Humperdink loved power and glory and had the right to choose any woman he desired. Despite the fact that she did not love him, the prince chose Buttercup for his bride, and they were to be wed at once. The people loved Buttercup. His plan was to get rid of Wesley and arranged to have his bride murdered on their honeymoon then blame the opposing kingdom, creating sympathy from the people to seek revenge in order to declare war and take over. War is good business, after all." I ended. Unfortunately, Byron wasn't convinced.

A few days later I called my cousin in Nassau and asked how things were going over there. She told me things were really slow as a result of the September 11th incident; employees were working three days a week, and that their straw market had burned down. "That's too bad. Hopefully things will pick up soon." I sympathized. Getting off the phone I thought, 'Well there go my plans.' I hadn't a plan B only a plan A and there was no way I was going back to Canada. Serena recommended I stay with Pearly and Corrina and see if they can help me get straight. I spoke with Pearly to see if it was ok that I come and stay with her. She obliged. I was excited because I'd never been to Dallas before and was looking forward to meeting Corrina and her daughter for the first time. So instead of leaving for the Bahamas I stayed in the U.S. and drove from Ft. Lauderdale to Dallas soon after the country was attacked and on orange alert.

In making preparations for my departure, I went to the library and photocopied a map of the southern States and followed the directions taking, I 95 north to Jacksonville then west on I 10 that stretches all the way to Houston then north on I 45 to Dallas. After I attended to the necessary car upkeep – a full tune up and oil change, I hit the road. Serena told me to be careful and call as soon as I reached Pearly's.

Driving out of Ft. Lauderdale, a vast gray cloud appeared. It rained modestly, blessing me for a few miles. When the rain stopped and the clouds cleared, I saw the most beautiful rainbow emerge from the sky to my far left. Surprisingly the rainbow's end was in the direction I was heading. God is good. I had been given a pot of gold. I felt like I hit da lotto. Naturally, I cranked up the music and began seat dancing.

Along the way I saw many U-Haul trucks pass by. I thought either a lot of people are moving out of Florida or it's just the same U-Haul trucks playing leap frog with me.

I made it to Mobile, Alabama before crashing at a motel for the night. The next morning I was up early and on the road again. Every now and then I'd see an armadillo lying by the side of the road. I thought to myself, 'Well girl, you're definitely not in Canada, otherwise you'd be seeing raccoons.'

I drove all the way to downtown Dallas before getting out of the car to use the payphone at a gas station. When Pearly answered, she said I'd gone too far and passed their place. So I went back up the highway and got off to meet her at the gas station where she said she'd be and then I followed her back to their apartment. When we arrived I met Corrina and her daughter Tina. Corrina and Tina were living with Pearly and her two children at the time.

I also met Corrina and Pearly's Ma and other kin and received real southern hospitality. I got on well with all of them except Cousin Leroy who was about my age. On our first meeting he asked "You one of them Germans ain't cha?" "You've obviously never been to Germany or know what a German accent sounds like. I'm from Canada. You're hearing a Canadian accent." "Oh Canada, you a half breed?" I found him endearing in an annoying kinda way.

I'd see Leroy every now and then at the house helping out or at family functions, saying things like, "Y'don't sound black. Wha y'know 'bout bein black bein raised in Canada?"

Why was this dim witted fool pressing my buttons? Most times I let it slide until that comment got me riled up. "Oh, y'wanna see the black a me come out? Y'don't wan dat, she's crazier than da white a me! I'm a Whylly.

Wha cha know bout dat, huh?" Then he said he's from the streets. "Wha cha know bout dat?" he challenged. "So am I." I lied. "Which street?" he scoffed. "Main Street. What difference does it make which street? Streets are streets." I debated. We were always sparring. Pearly and Corrina were amused by our bickering.

Because I couldn't work legally in Texas, I volunteered at the Methodist Hospital in Dallas, three days a week, Monday, Wednesday and Friday. I did it mostly because it gave me something to do while my sisters were at work and the kids in school, besides it felt good helping people.

Volunteering at the hospital was a gratifying experience yet made me feel like a square peg in a round hole, because the rest of the volunteers were retired seniors. Every time I came in, they'd look upon me with this question of 'Why are you here?' I repeatedly explained. "I'm doing it because I'm from Canada and I can't legally work here so I might as well make myself useful, while getting to know my family."

It's only natural that getting to know people takes time. Nevertheless, I am so pleased that I met all four of my sisters and was able to spend time getting to know them. God is good. God blessed me with; the four most beautiful, precious, kind and craziest women to be my sisters he/she could find.

Both Pearly and Corrina's birthdays are in November so they often have their party together. I was happy to be a part of the festivities. We brought fried catfish, barbequed chicken, meat balls, collard greens, rice n' peas, baked macaroni and cheese, Cole slaw, potato salad and birthday cake to the 'Gold Rush' night club for the celebration and decorated our reserved table with balloons. Pearly and Corrina's family and friends came and we had a blast eating, drinking, and pinning money on the birthday girls, while dancing to good music such as 'Living it up' by Ja Rule and having fun.

Another night I went out with a friend I met through Pearly. We were rollin around listening ta filthy sounds of da dirty south when I forgot my bank card in the machine because I was intoxicated and didn't notice until the next morning. I went back to the bank and spoke with a teller about retrieving it. She said that they don't keep any bank cards that don't belong to their bank. I was pissed to say the least. That meant I had no money. Because of it I stopped volunteering at the hospital to reserve gas and started thinking about returning to Canada. It was January 2002 and I still wasn't ready to face the Canadian winters. "You aint afraid of the threat of nuclear war?" my sister asked. The media was pumping more crap again. I didn't believe that would ever happen, so I answered "Nuclear war has nothing on Canadian winters. Winter scares me more."

I decided to stay until March and spent more time with them and the remaining time watching movies while everyone was out. I didn't watch much TV but there was one show that told stories about the unexplained. I think it was called 'Beyond Chance.' The show I remembered most was about a woman known for her gift of telepathy; She had always been a very shy, sensitive child and showed a picture of herself when she was a little girl with her dog. Animals were her only friends and she soon developed the ability to communicate with them.

There was a zoo in California that was experiencing trouble with their elephants. They weren't listening to the zookeepers and were becoming more and more disobedient. The zookeepers were at a loss as what to do about it. A co-worker referred the telepathic lady to the head zookeeper but he was skeptical about her abilities. Having seen no other options the head zookeeper decided to give the lady a chance. They arranged to have her come and meet with the elephants. When she arrived to greet them, the elephants immediately approached her. They all surrounded her giving her very little personal space. Then they put their trunks on her and began to sniff up and down her whole body. She described it as being examined by many vacuum hoses. Taking into account her being there to help them, she spoke to the elephant who was the matriarch. She said in the interview, that the matriarch was a wise being and explained to her that one of their family members had died recently. The matriarch said: "In order for us to have peace of mind, we must see the body and grieve which will bring closure. All beings that go through death must undergo all the steps of the grieving process to have peace of mind."

Following their meeting, she asked the head zookeeper about the death amongst the herd. He confirmed, "Yes, there was a death," much to his surprise. "Do you still have the body?" she asked. "No" he said. Dumbfounded that the woman knew about the dead elephant, he asked. "How could you have known?" No longer a skeptic he did inform her that they still had the skull, "Would that be enough?" "Yes" she replied. When the elephants viewed and caressed the skull of their beloved with their trunks, the transformation was instant. Amazingly, everything was back to normal and the elephants were very happy, as were the zookeepers. The elephants also received a better diet and nicer quarters. (Well if you have an interpreter you might as well communicate all your needs.)

In the spring of 2002, I drove back to Canada. It only took two days to reach the Buffalo border from Dallas while grooving to Ludacris and singing along, changing the words slightly to "...Move bitch, get out da way... get out da way while I smoke my Mary J..."

It was well past 11pm when I rolled up to the gate at customs. The lady at the booth asked, "Where are you coming from?" "Florida" I said passing her my I.D. "How long were you in Florida?" she questioned looking at it. "Two weeks." I said. She paused for a moment, (probably thinking whether or not to pull me aside and have me searched) then passed back my I.D. and said "Have a good night." I managed a smile and replied, "Thanks, you too." I drove away thinking, 'It's really been four months in Florida and six months in Texas; Ten months in total, again mixing the two T's, two and ten. Two weeks, ten months, ten weeks or two months. What difference does it make, time doesn't exist anyway.'

I stayed with Aunt Maureen's older sister, Aunt Irene and her husband Pat and their son Kevin until I got back on my feet. They lived in a small town an hour northwest of Toronto called Acton. Its claim to fame is the old hide house, a large store that sells leather and suede clothes, shoes, furniture and accessories. Therefore their slogan was 'It's worth the drive to Acton.' Mark was staying with them for a short time used to say, "It's worth the drive from Acton."

He moved out a month after I moved in. I kept busy cleaning houses, working at a retirement home and doing some background work in film.

Several months later, Kevin's daughter Nikki showed up. We didn't know why her mother dropped her off at her grandparents' house. Needless to say she was well received and Aunt Irene let her have Mark's old room. Nikki made friends at the local high school and even acquired a boyfriend. She spent most of her time with them and was given some leeway. When I did see her, she would compliment me on my outfits. I knew that meant she would be dipping in my closet when I wasn't around. I didn't mind. I don't recall anyone buying her new clothes for school, so I pretended not to notice any tops go missing, then reappear a few days later.

Nikki was sitting at the kitchen counter watching me prepare dinner. "You're strange." she said. "You have no idea." I smiled at her. Aunt Irene and Uncle Pat agreed that was a compliment coming from a teenager. I didn't care what she meant by it. She probably wondered why I never confronted her about infringing on my personal space. That didn't matter to me I was more concerned with her well being. I sensed a deep sadness in her at times. I'd ask her about school and if she missed her friends. She admitted she did, but was making friends at her new school. I don't recall her bringing any of them over to the house, just the boyfriend who I met a couple of times. It was obvious they were having sex. I saw scabs on the top of her feet one night while we were watching TV. The funny thing is... I knew only because at thirty-three I was doing the same thing; Doing it in the back seat of a car, girl on top, with the feet rubbing against the fabric creating rug burn. I had the same scabs on my feet but I wore socks so no one could see. Having her in my life made me wonder if I was ever going to grow up or be ready for parenthood. I knew she needed guidance but what kind of guidance could I give her, when I needed guidance myself?

By the summer of 2003, the song 'Cleaning out my closet' by Eminem was heard continuously from Nikki's room. "...I'm sorry Mama I never meant to hurt you. I never meant to make you cry, but tonight I'm cleaning out my closet..." She invited me in to show how clean her room was. It turns out she was cleaning out her closet. I took her to see the movie '8 Mile' starring the rap artist when it was in theatres. We made plans to go to Canada's Wonderland, and started spending more time together. I had hoped that going out might do her good, especially after she and her boyfriend were spending less time together since the summer started. I guess he wanted to explore other relationships. Wallowing about it, she spent more time sleeping in, and then lounged on the couch watching TV all day. Aunt Irene gave her a kitten hoping it would cheer her up. I reminded her that she was young and to have fun. "There'll be lots of opportunities to meet other guys." I told her. Though, my words weren't encouraging.

One afternoon Nikki came into the kitchen dressed up like Mortisha from the Adams family. Her long, wet brown hair was slick back giving it an even darker appearance. Her face was painted white and she was wearing black lipstick, black eyeliner and black nail polish. "Is that your new look? Do you want to be dead?" I teased. Nikki merely smiled at me.

A few days later, I talked her into coming with me to see our cousin Mark, who lived in Hamilton. The drive was a scenic one because I took the side roads. It was nice hanging with Nikki. Along the way, I asked questions. I asked her what her ambition in life was and what she wanted to be when she grew up. She wasn't interested in anything, she told me. When we reached Mark's apartment he wasn't home. He wanted me to bring her the next time I came around. He didn't know we were coming. It was suppose to be a surprise. We sat on the curb talking, Nikki and I, then left after waiting awhile.

The following weekend everyone had plans to be somewhere except Nikki. Sunday evening, everyone returned home and we sat around the kitchen table eating dinner and discussed current events and how everyone's weekend went. "Where's Nikki?" Aunt Irene inquired. No one knew, probably over at her friend's house, we all assumed. Looking at the time, I excused myself from the table while they were still eating. Aunt Irene asked if I would be so kind as to put Shorty back in Nikki's room. Acknowledging her request, I scooped up the little fur ball then trotted down the stairs and entered her room.

Conclusion

I was sitting in my car in front of the library, building the nerve to go in. But every time I blinked my eyes, I could see Nikki's blue face, while the powerful words of 'Sunday bloody Sunday', played endlessly in my head. My whole world collapsed and the only awareness I attained was the song, as numbness crept in, little by little until I became completely paralyzed. Surrendering to it, I sat there. I sat for hours...

Coming out of the trance, I noticed the sun was beginning to set and the library was closed for the day. Gradually, I regained enough mental and physical strength to start the car. In the twilight, I could still see her blue face every time I blinked. I drove out of the library parking lot then down the street. Wiping the tears away, I could not understand why this happened. Why did she do it? Why am I experiencing another suicidal death? Why did I have to see her dead body? The experience was more than I could bear.

Traumatized, I feared that I might not ever recover, constantly seeing her blue face and frightened that I may be permanently scarred for life. I became exceedingly angry with God because I was told he/she would not give anyone more than they can handle. I thought life was supposed to be easier not harder. The more I thought about it, the angrier I got. Seething, I became livid and wanted to know why. So I pounded the steering wheel with my fists and I yelled at God saying "What kind of all knowing, all loving being are you for putting me through this? This is not funny, you sick fuck! I demand to know and I demand to know Right NOW!!"

Instantly, I received a picture in my mind of 'Beyond Chance' the television show I happened to see while visiting my sisters in Texas; The story about the unruly elephants at the zoo and the telepathic lady that came to help them. They needed to see their loved one's body that the zookeepers took away, in order to complete their grieving process which would bring peace of mind. They needed closure. I needed closure. That's all; Closure on my mother's death as I did not get to see her body. But how could I after her cremation? Instead, I received closure from grieving over Nikki's body. Eighteen years had gone by since my mom died; all those years searching for answers, when all I needed was closure. That's why I had the dream about death, to prepare me for the inevitable. Once I fully understood what God was communicating to me, I realized.

It was the greatest gift in disguise.

In conclusion, time heals and reveals and whenever we ask for guidance, it is given. I know my mom loved me

Bibliography & Discography

Chanoine C. Barthas and Pere G. Da Fonseca, S.J. Our Lady of Light. The Bruce Publishing Company, U.S.A. (seventh printing -1950)*

U2 – Sunday Bloody Sunday – 1983 Album, War.

Toni Basil – Mickey – 1982 Album, Word of Mouth.

Depeche Mode – Blasphemous Rumors – 1984 Album, Some Great Reward.

The Nylons – Kiss Him Goodbye – 1987 Album, Happy Together.

Ludacris – Move Bitch – 2001 Album, Word of Mouf.

Eminem – Cleaning out my closet -2002 Album, The Eminem show.

An Excerpt From

How to Have Fun with God

A guide to a richer and fuller life

It was August 2007 when the man in black revisited me. Only this time, I wasn't asleep, nor was I dreaming. I was wide awake. It happened in broad daylight, around three in the afternoon, after I came home from work. He appeared floating towards me, waving his arms as if trying to scare me and even though he didn't anymore, I was disturbed by his presence. This spectacle went on every day for almost a week before I started to write about the dream, where the man in black and I first met. Each day that passed as I wrote about him, he began to fade away. Until one day I just kept on writing and the man in black faded away completely...